KAIO PUBLICATIONS, INC.

Visit www.kaiopublications.org
for more valuable resources.

Football the Piggy teaches us about Love
Written by The Wells Family
Illustrated by Jessica Benavides
Edited by Erin McDonald
Graphic Design by Elisa Elmshaeuser
Please do not make any reproductions of any kind
without the express written consent of the author and the illustrator.
Copyright ©2016 by Kaio Publications, Inc.

Football the Piggy
teaches us about

LOVE

By The Wells Family

Illustrated by Jessica Benavides

Once upon a time, in a land far, far away there lived a piggy, named Football.

He was a joyful little guy who loved going on great adventures, and today he was going on an extra special adventure.

Football woke up early this morning, even before Ranger the Rooster, because he wanted to get an early start.

After he changed out of his pajamas and into his overalls, made his bed, and brushed his teeth, he rushed downstairs to join his parents at the breakfast table.

"Good morning, mom! Good morning, dad!" Football cheerfully said.

"Good morning, my beautiful son!" Mama Pig replied as she smiled back at him.

His father, Papa Pig, looked up from his morning paper and gave him a soft pat on the top of his head, as if to say, "I'm very proud of you."

"If it's OK with you both, after breakfast, I would like to go over to Fletcher the Fox's house, and see if we can go to the fair," Football said.

After receiving permission from his parents, Football finished his breakfast and hurried out the door. He ran through the gate, down the sidewalk, and all the way to Fletcher's house.

Knock, Knock, Knock...

Football waited patiently for Fletcher to come to the door.

"Hi Fletcher!" smiled Football.

"My parents said I can go to the fair today, can you come with me?" he asked hopefully.

Fletcher rushed to ask Papa and Mama Fox if he could join Football at the fair. After a very short time, he came back to the door with his favorite hat on his head.

"They said YES!" Fletcher replied excitedly with a big smile.

The two friends rushed out of the gate and down the sidewalk, skipping toward the fairgrounds.

After seeing the Ferris wheel high in the sky above the trees, hearing all the other boys and girls having fun, and smelling all the wonderful food, all they could think about was getting there as quickly as their little legs could run.

Just as they rounded the last turn, they came to a screeching halt. Sitting on the sidewalk, with her head in her hands, sat July the Jaguar crying.

"July, what's wrong? Are you alright? Are you hurt?" asked Football very concerned.

Sniff, Sniff...

"Oh, hi Football and Fletcher," July replied. "My tire popped on my bike, and I fell down. My knee hurts a lot. I can't walk."

Looking at the bike, then turning back to look at July, Football said, "I am so sorry you are hurt. You really should get home so your parents can look at your knee. You may need to go see the doctor."

"I know, I just don't think I can get home," July said, as more tears began to run down her face.

Football looked over at Fletcher, and the two of them knew what they needed to do. The fair must wait because their friend needed help.

"We'll help you get home," Football said. "One of us can push your bike home and the other can help hold you up. If we get tired along the way, we can switch."

"Oh, you will do that for me?" July, asked unsure of why the two of them would do that. "You were both running fast. Weren't you headed for the fair?"

"We were," Fletcher said. "But there are some things even more important than the fair, and when we see someone who is hurt and in need, the fair doesn't seem all that important anymore."

"Now let's get you home," Football said, helping July to her feet.

As July put her arm around Football's neck, Fletcher picked up the bicycle, and the three of them began the long walk to her house.

Across the bridge and through the park the three walked, only pausing long enough to switch who was pushing the bicycle and who was helping July.

Seeing them approach, July's mother ran out of the front door. "What happened? Are you hurt?"

July hugged Mama Jaguar and said, "I was riding my bike to the fair, and the tire popped. I fell hard to the ground and hurt my knee." Her eyes began to tear up as she told her mother what had happened.

"Football and Fletcher were running to the fair. When they saw me on the sidewalk, they stopped to check on me. Instead of going to the fair, they decided to help," said July thankfully.

"Boys, I can't tell you how grateful I am that you chose to help," Mama Jaguar said. "We will go inside so I can look at that knee. We may need to go to the doctor to get it checked."

After taking July inside her house, Football and Fletcher began walking back toward their own houses, realizing they didn't have time to get to the fair.

"When I woke up this morning, I had in mind what I was going to do," said Football. "I was sure by this time I would have already ridden the Ferris wheel at least three times and the merry-go-round twice, but I know it was more important to help July. There'll be other chances to go to the fair."

Fletcher chimed in, "I know what you mean. I was so excited when you asked me this morning to come with you, but July needed us. We couldn't just leave her on the sidewalk hurting."

As they walked back through the park and over the bridge, reaching their houses, Football said goodbye to Fletcher, and the two of them parted ways.

"How was the fair?" mother asked Football.

"We didn't make it," he replied.

Papa Pig was sitting in the chair, and looked up from his book.

"Why? Did something happen?" he asked, concerned.

"No, sir. I mean, yes, sir," Football stumbled.

"What happened, honey?" Mama Pig asked.

Football began telling his
mom and dad everything
that happened.

Placing his hand on Football's head, Papa Pig said, "I am very proud of you, son."

Smiling, Football looked at his father.

"You decided to not do what you really wanted so that you could help your friend who was hurt," his father lovingly said. "You could have kept going and passed her over, but you didn't. That tells me a lot. You showed that you are a person of compassion and love."

Football, not understanding everything his father said, asked, "What do you mean, daddy?"

"You see, when a person decides to put aside what they want to do or what's important to them, like spending the day at the fair, so that they can help others in need, that's called love," his father explained. "It's this kind of love that God showed us when He sent Jesus to die on the cross so we could one day live in heaven with Him, and it's this kind of love we are supposed to have as we follow God."

"We are so proud of you, Football" his mom said as she hugged her son.

That night as Football was in bed, he thought about what his father had said. As he thought about the lessons he had learned in Bible class about Jesus, he smiled, grateful for the love God shows him, his family, and his friends. He then drifted off to sleep.

The next morning, Football woke up, changed out of his pajamas and into his overalls, made his bed, and brushed his teeth. As he made his way down the stairs to the breakfast table, he was greeted by his parents.

"Good morning, my beautiful son," Mama Pig said, smiling.

Papa Pig reached over and put his hand on Football's head like he always did.

"Are you ready to go?" his dad asked.

"Go where? Where are we going?" Football replied.

"To the fair, of course!" his father said as a big grin came across his face. "We thought that since you missed it yesterday, we would go today as a family."

Football rushed out of his chair and gave his father and mother great big hugs.

"We love you, sweetheart," Mom and Dad said lovingly.

"I love you, too," Football happily replied.

The End

CPSIA information can be obtained
at www.ICGtesting.com
Printed in the USA
LVHW071049151021
700536LV00002B/16

9 780996 043045